Grieving
Healing
Accepting

25 Sympathy Poems of Loss

Ann Vincent Vila

Library of Congress Control Number: 2020914131
Subjects: Poetry – Grief
Printed in the United States of America
Photographs by the Artist & Poet, Ann Vincent Vila

First Edition
ISBN: 978-1-7354213-0-8

For information contact Publisher:
Anna Gossett Johnson
annaj526@gmail.com
Burbank, California

10 9 8 7 6 5 4 3 2 1

A Personal Note:

My deepest and sincerest condolences
for your irreplaceable loss. May you find
some comfort in these pages.

Ann Vincent Vila

Dedication

This book is dedicated to
the memory of my husband, Russell.

Along with his passing, there are also poems
that speak to all of my experiences with the
concept of Loss.

Lastly, this book is dedicated to all those,
like myself, who have lost someone and now
grieve, heal and accept every day that Loss.

Ann Vincent Vila
Burbank, California, 2020

Table of Contents

Grieving

Night Sky

It is those moments of clarity
where everything becomes too clear

where the sun burns my eyes
through sun glasses

where my head itches under my sun hat
melting in a Los Angeles heat wave
of desperation.

Where I just wish I could turn the corner
and find you waiting there again

smiling and laughing at me for feeling lost,
but there is no street where I can find you.

There is no phone that can ever
reach you again.

The stars have rolled you up in Heaven
and the only way I can see you

is when I gaze at the night sky
and see you breathing as a star.

Loss

is what calls me.
It begs me to remember
remember, remember
what I wish to forget.
There is a sputtering cloud
that lives above my head
and yet my kitchen is sunny
as light filters in each day,
while greyness lingers
my mind enmeshed in
loss.

I Heard

On the phone I heard
"dead, died."
After that nothing.
Smothering blanket of silence
covered my throbbing head.

Could only think
last time we spoke
laughed and joked.
Waiter brought drinks
toasted memories and time.

But understanding
finally the void you left
like a vacant house
once lived within now
just shadows remain.

.

As The Sun Sets

Just how quickly
light filters
painting my pillows
in streaks of yellow
like memory
staining the present
only to fade
with time
as the sun sets
brightest
before it flees
into night.
I am a witness.
You were here
but now
gone.

Regret

Whatever darkness overtook
you, I try to understand

now what deafening Circe
song lured you.

Then, I had no eyes to see.
your thoughts yelling

as with a megaphone
ear splitting self-hate.

As we laughed, joking
drinking, I had no idea

aching wounds you hid
and felt, only thinking

of myself. Trying to
impress with yellow lies.

I, a vacant shell, no safe
or calming harbor for you.

Only when I awoke blurry
as a voice spoke on the phone,

"I'm sorry, He died this morning,"
I realized I hadn't heard you.

Now stomach aches
throbbing red shame and regret.

Somehow I'd forgotten to
look in your eyes and listen.

Phone Keeps Ringing

Sympathy oozes out of the phone like honey
onto skin. Keeps ringing. My tongue

throbs mute.

What do I say? *He is dead. He died. I'm alone.*

Silence like a vacant movie theatre.
Everyone

scatters.

Left alone in the dark. Workers with their brushes,
buckets and me sitting there alone in

the dark.

Time to go. But where now? What's home?
Empty egg carton where eggs once lived.

Without

you, no longer a home more an empty
carton of milk thrown away. Phone keeps

ringing reminds me

wake up.

A Ritual

Back seat of my Toyota,
I grasp the strings of rainbow

colored balloons as a torch.
Grieving ritual, Griffith Park.

Climbing we pick a trail
once hiked as family years

ago before illness mangled
your tortured inflamed body.

We have no ashes with us.
This is no site for them, but rather

an Arcadia of remembrance.
We listen to Enya as balloons

become confetti in clear azure
sky fluttering higher and higher

climbing until gone, vanishing.
Gazing beguiled by the heavens.

At home, as your ghost hovers,
we eat your favorite treat: Pizza Hut

Large Pepperoni with Diet Coke,
savoring the last essence of you.

Never Accept

I will never accept
your dying so young.

Laughter was still
upon your lips and Spring

still gleamed within
your eyes of days yet to be.

So how is it now
that you are so deep

within the dewy ground
lost to us forever.

Dearest do you stroll
the graveyard at night?

A beaming spirit that lurks
these stones enchanted

upon the moonlight?
If this is true, one day

I'll catch your shadow
and see you once again

to curse the dreaded night
for taking you too early.

A Temporary Gift

A pet's love:
Nothing lacking
gentle presence.
Tender eyes seeking.
No games, no agendas.
Purest love:
No lies or betrayal.
Only wagging tails
or gentle purring.
When pets die,
hurt scars the heart.
Hollow ache
in your core.
A temporary gift
on loan
with love
to last a lifetime.

Loss of a Pet

There
is a deep loss
for the loss of a pet
that not everyone
can understand
for
special people have
rare places in
their Hearts
where
Sweet pets find a place
to be loved.

Home For The Holidays

Holidays unique silken twine
twists, binds, cuts my heart,

upon banter, secret world
a family culture.

Belly laughter, tears,
ingrained teasing. Distinctive:

Unusual – one
of a kind.

Mystery of Christmas trees.
Caress ornaments, Sing Holiday

songs. Grieve the unspoken:
a look, smile.

Joyful agony, begin inhaling
memory seeping seasonal aromas

turkey, and pumpkin pie
that ache of days lost.

Disregarding all messy truths.
Aching to right all wrongs.

Ghosts hover. Swallow reverie
sipping egg nog.

Vanished

Husky
breathing

presence
of you as a person

strong, holding
my hand.

I never understood
that grasp of warmth

until you
vanished

as in the air
whipping my skin

as you
floated away

now
as ashes

thrown to the
sea.

Healing

Voyage Back Home

The unexpected phone call
crashing loss

silence
seeps into the trudging of

everyday life. Voyage
back home

to view each room with
a cloud of absence,

quiet.
They have gone. Are

gone. Between wails
of grief.

Details. Voices now lost
in sobbing childhood

wild tears.
Papers to be signed.

Decisions: burial, ashes.
Gruesome.

Numbing tedium
process. Robot like,

Hello, Goodbye.
Then like a spirit's whisper,

*Remember, Remember
to live.*

Morning Sky

I see you as a morning sky
when the clouds are whispering

white brush strokes on a canvas
of hazy light blue.

I hear you as doves coo
their morning song

bringing their twigs building nests
in our pots of pink and white geraniums.

Your scent lingers in the sofa
of balm offered for comfort

as cancer pains struck
inflaming your body.

Your pictures throughout
the house remind me

there once was a world
of love I knew.

You are here
every moment of the day,

waiting patiently nearby
for me one day to pass

through an invisible lighted
doorway into your arms.

Come to Me

Come to me
when I am lost

on an endless highway searching
needing to hear your voice
just one more time.

Come to me
upon awakening each dawn

to unsung promises of the sun
you by my side
just one more time.

Come to me
knowing your ashes are gone

spread along a sacred road trip.
Yet, wishing you near
just one more time.

Come to me: To venture back,
To taste a Montana sky,

To hear the prairie wind sing
whispering your essence
just one more time.

Treasures

We survived on laughter.
It fed us.

No real money just illusions
and dreams

were enough to stomach those
hard years:

An empty refrigerator, one
good meal,

a rattling car that barely ran, somehow
kept going.

How is it now those years seem like
red jewels

that I take down and polish as my
treasures.

Salvation

I find my eyes pressed closed
bowing over candles

lit by sorrow.
The quiet of the

church, sacred
still and hushed

mournfully dark
secretive therein.

Dark wood
stabbing my knees

as I kneel offering
petitions for mercy

as candles
flicker their lament

that life now
a dulled grey fog

somehow
led me here

where solace
survives.

Goodbye

There has to be
a way to say goodbye

like lighting candles in church
praying you can somehow still
hear me.

There has to be
a way to say goodbye

like placing your name on a park bench
wishing as I touch your name I can somehow still
reach you.

There has to be
a way to say goodbye

like sky writing your name
on the clearest blue sky to somehow reach you in
Heaven.

There has to be
a way to say goodbye

as suddenly you are dead and
my voice echoes in the void left by your
Silence.

.

Winter

Love that I once had it
wide eyes, warm mouth

that I once felt loved
long gone, dead now.

Arrived a surprise
a door opened

then a path to follow
then left as fast.

Like a summer season
turns burning hot

until autumn gold appears
then winter chills.

Love taunts me still
like fog baffling me

clouding my day
with blinding snow.

Accepting

Alive

Alive
within me you
go on
and provoke me

to move forward
when I
want to stop and
give up.

But you murmur
through the
wind. Trees
whisper your

voice
as I bow
gently and
persist.

Today

Today stings of yesterday's
loss: kisses, hugs, warmth
and yet

the golden memory
of you hovers near
somehow

loving me, helping me
move on as I mourn you
each day.

Whirling above clouds
as stolen beauty, I
once knew.

The sky like a doorway
holds inexplicable
secrets.

As if to treasure
love, first, we must
lose it.

The Passage Way

Tears and grief, but
knowing your stinging

agony over easier to
accept:

To not see your
purple darkened face

body aching
enflamed.

To not see your
frantic night gathering

of things as for some
venture.

To not hear you
cry in the night. Yelling

as to a destined waiting
new land.

To not see your
lost gaze, no longer seeing

me but somehow looking
beyond.

As when night overtook
you, I knew your torment

had ceased upon
passage.

Your Essence

You are here
lingering between

pages of favorite books
waving to me from our
bookcase.

Let others think
you're gone. They're not

aware of finger prints
left as a pattern on
my heart.

Your spirit
never gone but always

here. For whenever I need you
somehow your scent
finds me.

As though near,
dawn awakens me.

Its warm rays
like your arms calm
my soul.

Stony Cliffs

To grieve
is to heal.

It's
a path

upon
stony cliffs

darkened
passages

to a
dawning

sun of
acceptance.

Loss is
real

but love
endless.

To heal
we must be

willing first
to grieve.

Resilience

Yet, Green buds
grow

within me

meandering
a forest.

Gasping
unsullied air.

Every breath
revives each cell.

I, as a particle
of life, fluent

across time
face mortality

clutching
irreversibly

your memory
as life's beauty,

resilient.

Final Notes

Thank you for buying this book. This is a sympathy gift book of poetry from my heart to anyone who needs comfort. From my own experience, I have found that the act of grieving is a healing process. As a poet and artist, I make no claims as a physician or a medical professional. My knowledge is empirical from my own loss. Although I planned this book long before the Pandemic, that sorrow acted as the final catalyst for me to share the poems with those now grieving.

Although we all know nothing can bring back those we have lost, it is that final acceptance that in some sense heals. For as long as we remember and cherish the memory of those we have loved, they live within us forever. I might suggest that you find one poem within the volume and memorize it to comfort you in those moments that cause renewed pain, as the act of reciting it may soothe your heart. I would suggest the very last poem, *Resilience*, as a possible choice for this.

Please feel free to write me through the email provided by the publisher. I send these poems out into the universe hoping they help in some small way.

Blessings and Peace to all,
Ann Vincent Vila

Made in the USA
Las Vegas, NV
11 July 2022

51371278R00038